THE LITTLE BOOK ON BIG EGO

JOEL EPSTEIN

A Guide to Manage and Control The Egomaniacs in Your Life

The Little Book on BIG EGO

To order additional copies of this title,
visit www.frictionfactor.net or call 877-EGO-MAN1.

The author may be contacted at the following address:

Friction Factor
11400 Rockville Pike, Suite 280
Rockville, MD 20852

Phone: 301-821.6585, fax: 301-816-9814
Email: joel@frictionfactor.net
Website: www.frictionfactor.net

Jacket Design by Amy J. Etcheson
Page Design by Maryland Composition
Printed in Landover, Maryland by Mount Vernon Printing

ISBN 10: 0-9787059-0-4
ISBN 13: 978-0-9787059-0-9

Acknowledgments

I live my life by the following theory:

"One's success or failure in life depends on who we meet, AND what we do about it when we meet them."

Meaning, I try to live my life as a sponge. I want to learn as much from every person that I meet along the way. My theory is really all about ego. My ego. When I interact with people I always assume I can learn something new from them. I know that I can learn from every single person I meet, and I try to do so. Sometimes I learn something new to do; other times I learn what not to do. So in reality, I have a WHOLE lot of people to thank regarding this book. This is The Little Book on Big Ego, so I'll make it as short and to the point as possible.

I have to start at the beginning and thank my wonderful parents, Bob and Gail

ACKNOWLEDGMENTS

Epstein. Then, of course, people met and befriended along the way, Pat Casey, Marc Smith, Todd Duncan, Greg Frost, Tom Fiddler, Dave Zadareky, Bill Gross, Jay Abraham, Carolyn Bobb, and Erika Zabell, my lucky charm.

Last, but not least, the person who helped make my dream a reality, my burrito brother, Terry Hart.

For

Alec, Noah, and Lauren

Why is this "The Little Book On Big Ego"? Why isn't it 300 pages? Because egos don't flare, explode, and damage slowly over 300 pages. When egos explode, they explode instantly.

It might take a big book to understand the causes of overheated and over-inflated egos, but this book isn't about curing destructive human behavior. We'll leave that to psychiatrists. This book is about you controlling an explosive ego situation and turning that potentially disastrous encounter into a neutral experience or even a positive result.

To learn to control an exploding ego doesn't take a big book or a lot of time either. Controlling and managing an egomaniac, can happen as quickly as the initial, irrational ego explosion.

Let egos explode, you and everyone loses. When you read this little book, you'll be able to do big things because when you manage and control the egomaniacs in your life you win.

TABLE OF CONTENTS

The Facts About Friction

Ego is the foundation for tremendous achievement, success, and leadership.

Ego is the cornerstone of deals not closed, ruined relationships, and failed careers.

Ego can be your strongest ally, or your worst enemy.

Strong, healthy egos build careers, businesses, and lives. Inflated, out of control egos will destroy it all.

EGO MONSTERS

What is an Ego Monster? An Ego Monster is an Egomaniac. Ego Monsters are people who think the world revolves around them. Ego Monsters don't care much for the feelings of others. Ego Monsters have Ego Flares (negative criticism, a demeaning statement, or a taunt) and are capable of starting an Ego Fire (an argument, a loud disagreement, or a fight) almost every time they open their mouths. Ego Monsters love to cause trauma, not to mention drama. Ego Monsters can be mean, or very nice (on the outside), loud or calm. You run into Ego Monsters everyday. They're everywhere. They're people you know. They're total strangers. In your own house, at the coffee shop, family gatherings, at the gas station, in school, at your child's soccer game, and especially in your office. In the business world, virtually every problem, up to, and including failed business ventures, is due to someone's ego "getting in the way." This little book will teach you how to recognize the Ego Monsters in your life, and how to manage and control them. This book will show you how to put out an Ego Fire, and also how to prevent an Ego Fire from occurring.

We may never really know what makes a person's ego explode and turn them into an Ego Monster. The thing to understand is, we can't change this person. What we can do is effectively manage and control the individual we are dealing with along with his ego. Calming a raging ego and getting your desired result from this encounter is what you want. And you can get what you want, even if the other person is a raging Ego Monster.

Everyone has an ego. Ego is a ball of energy. Every ego is the same size. No one's ego is bigger, smaller, wider, or thinner than anyone else's. They're all the same. The difference is how our ego is affected and how we react.

Your ego (ball of energy) can be affected positively or negatively by many things. If you subject your ego to different environments, inputs, and situations, your ego (and you), will not react the same way to each situation. People look at the world in different ways, not "right" or "wrong," just differently. How we view and react to situations creates either Positive or Negative Friction, which affects our egos. A negatively affected ego always creates some type of Ego Monster. Different personality types will result in different types of Ego Monsters. They might be cocky. They could be angry, mean and argumentative. They could be jealous or competitive. They might be loud Ego Monsters or quiet ones. The point is, you don't care about "why" they are that way. You care about the "how", as in, "How do I deal with this Ego Monster?"

FRICTION FACTORS

When an ego rubs against another person's ego, it creates friction. Most people automatically assume that friction between two people is negative, but that's not true. When people are passionate enough to disagree, there's always the potential for an improved result. A disagreement, when handled correctly, almost always results in a better solution for the challenge at hand. No friction typically means you're surrounded by "yes men" and success will be hard to come by. The question is, "When friction is created, is that friction going to be positive or negative—and are you going to succeed or fail?"

NEGATIVE FRICTION: Two or more egos rubbing up against each other to create a fire that burns wildly and out of control, therefore scarring, burning and frequently obliterating everything and everyone in its path.

POSITIVE FRICTION: Two or more egos rubbing up against each other to create a fire that is quickly controlled, then focused to be used to create more energy, which becomes an incredible thought, idea, or solution.

Everyday there are pivotal moments when you can turn a potentially disastrous ego situation (Negative Friction) into a positive and successful result (Positive Friction) just by recognizing and understanding the Friction Factor that's at play.

Some of the Friction Factors you will read about are specific actions you can take to calm a raging Ego Monster. Other Friction Factors are situations and motives behind an Ego Monster's irrational actions that, when recognized, give you an understanding of what's happening and why it's happening. This recognition will allow you to react correctly and calm an Ego Monster.

Friction is energy. Is the friction negative energy? If so, how do you turn it into Positive Friction so you can affect a successful outcome? Do you need more wood for the fire, or a bucket of water to put out the fire fast and prevent a disaster?

THE INFORMATION TRAFFIC COP

Everyone has an Information Traffic Cop. This little person is the first one to hear information as it enters the ear. The Information Traffic Cop takes this input, which can be anything from "Is that a new shirt?" to "Your idea is moronic and you're an idiot," and sends it to one of two places. All statements are either sent to the brain, or the ego. If the information goes to the brain for processing, you will be able to turn the statement into Positive Friction because the brain uses logic and intelligence. If, however, the Information Traffic Cop sends the input to the ego, we have a problem—the Negative Friction will most likely turn into more Negative Friction and possibly an Ego Explosion, because the ego uses emotion and anger. Is it really that simple? Absolutely.

Somebody says, "Bill, nice to see you. What's with the orange t-shirt? Kinda loud, don't you think?" The "kinda loud, don't you think" remark can be seen as a rude statement. If the Information Traffic Cop sends this statement to the brain the person will react by saying "Does my shirt really look that stupid?" Or he might just ignore the statement. If the statement goes to the ego, an Ego Flare is almost guaranteed, and that Ego Flare is the beginning of a full-fledged Ego Fire.

You're probably saying, "But I'd never say something unpleasant like that." Okay, but what if that statement was made to someone, and that someone's Information Traffic Cop sent the remark to the person's ego and an Ego Monster was born? . . . Then, you happen to be the next person that Ego Monster comes into contact with. You might not have anything to do with an Exploding Ego, but you're the recipient of the Ego Monster's wrath.

Another example of a common, seemingly innocent moment turning into an Ego Flare: The Boss is sitting behind his desk. An Employee comes in and says, "I was thinking about the process we use—we put A and B together and make C, then do D and get E. What if we just put A & D together, we'd get to E much faster."

The Boss is listening, hopefully, but what is the Boss thinking? All too often the Boss's Information Traffic Cop sends this conversation to his ego instead of his brain. The Boss's ego is thinking, "This rookie thinks he knows my business better than I do. What makes him think he can come in my office and tell me how to run my business that I built from scratch with my bare hands?" Now, the Boss may not be saying this out loud, but inside he's thinking it, consciously or maybe even subconsciously.

So, the Boss either ignores the Employee's suggestion or maybe lets his ego really take over, turns into an Ego Monster and the well-meaning interaction becomes a very unpleasant encounter. As a result, this idea, which maybe was good, maybe not, never even got a chance.

If an Ego Fire starts, the relationship between the Employee and the Boss will be damaged. Do you think that Employee will go to the Boss the next time he has an idea?

That was a Friction Factor moment and either the Boss or the Employee could have easily used the Friction Factors and turned the Negative Friction into Positive Friction. One or both of them could have turned the Negative Friction into Positive Friction and created a focused flame to then build a fire that could have improved the company process and benefited everyone.

The Information Traffic Cop sending information to the brain or the ego is simple. What isn't as simple is how to deal with the Ego Monsters when they're using their egos more often than their brains. Using the 10 Friction Factors will make dousing an Ego Fire or managing and controlling an Ego Monster much, much easier.

NEW? NO. POWERFUL AND EFFECTIVE? YES.

You might instinctively be aware and even use some of the Friction Factors we're about to discuss. I don't claim to have created new concepts that have never been thought of before. My goal is to have you focus on these principles and consciously use them in your daily encounters when Ego Flares occur or Ego Monsters are attacking.

This book is meant to be simple to read and to the point, but there is a deeper more meaningful reality to always keep in mind. When you manage and interact with people, whether it's in the business world or your personal life, you're managing and interacting with their egos as well. This means you have a great responsibility. It's not merely an Ego Monster you're dealing with. You're dealing with another human being. Egos are attached to pride. When a person's ego and pride are wounded it deeply affects them. You must sincerely care that a person's ego is healthy. You don't have to cure the psychological cause of an out of control Ego Monster being released, but taming an Ego Monster will enable that person to be more productive, more secure, and significantly more open with you, which means everyone wins.

Controlling and managing egos should not be viewed as a short-term, manipulative trick. Egos are pride based—we all have a responsibility to treat another person's ego as we want our ego to be treated, for everyone's short and long-term success.

Friction Factor

1

All Friction Is Good

*"Honest differences are often a healthy
sign of progress"*

MAHATMA GANDHI

"There's really friction between those two!" Everyone who hears that automatically assumes the friction is bad or negative. People confuse friction between individuals as an ego problem, or two egos "clashing." We're programmed to think all friction is bad, but when someone disagrees with you, you should never jump to the conclusion that it's negative. Assuming all friction is negative is lighting the fuse to an Ego Fire. Ego is like dynamite, and sure, dynamite can be explosive and dangerous, but when handled properly, dynamite can produce wonderfully positive results.

In the beginning, friction between two or more people is always good. The reason friction is always good is because friction is passion—and passion is very good. Who gets mad when there's no passion? When there's no passion, there's little or nothing to be gained.

The fact that there's a disagreement and friction is what usually leads to the best possible result. A passionate disagreement, when handled correctly, frequently results in a great solution for the challenge at hand or a creative new idea. Never view any type of friction as a negative. Use the energy for a positive result. If the friction isn't controlled, it can quickly turn from potentially Positive Friction, to Negative Friction, then to an Ego Fire that rages and wipes out every thing, every person, and every good thought within its reach.

So if there's passion and friction, the question is, do you have the ability to turn that passion into a positive result, or are you going to let it escalate into complete negativity?

Understanding that "All Friction Is Good" is the foundation to controlling and managing egos therefore, always increasing the odds of success.

I know you've been in this situation before. You're in a meeting where people are supposed to be working together to figure something out, to solve a problem, or to create a new way to do something—and two people disagree. If the person running the meeting, or the two competing people, let the disagreement turn into Negative Friction, which then can turn into a raging fire, nothing will be accomplished. When egos cause Negative Friction someone has to step in and say, "Hold it. There has to be something good here. There has to be a great idea here somewhere."

We all know people who've been through a divorce. Did the couple fight all the time? Maybe, but frequently they never fought. What that often means is there was never any passion, never any passionate disagreement there to even fight about. As a result they never came up with a better solution or improved situation. It was just, "I don't care," which in itself is a form of Negative Friction. What frequently happens, especially in office politics and personal lives is these type of disagreements become seeds that create horrible environments if they're not handled and managed correctly.

If you have an idea and you present it, and say, "The sky is blue." Then another person says, "The sky is pink." You might say, "The sky isn't pink, the sky is blue. I said it was blue." The pink guy says, "No, I said it's pink. The sky is pink." We now have Negative Friction that could potentially turn into an Ego Fire and burn everything in sight. My contention is, if you say the sky is blue and the person next to you says the sky is pink, instead of disagreeing with them, say, "That's interesting. Why do you say the sky is pink?" That simple change of response immediately creates an environment for Positive Friction instead of Negative Friction. If you say to a person, "Okay, you're an idiot for saying the sky is pink, it's obviously blue," you're going to have a negative reaction and nothing is going to get done.

Let's take another specific example . . .

You're in a meeting and there are ten people, five from the painting department and five from the wheel department. Someone says, "Here's the new way we're going to make our widget. We're going to paint it first, and then we're going to put the wheels on it." Someone from the other department says, "What? You can't put the wheels on after you paint it, you can't do that. That's impossible. That will never work." "Yes you can." "No you can't." We have an Ego Flare and it could easily turn into a full-blown Ego Fire.

Because one side has always done it their way, when someone else suggests a new or different way to do it, the person hearing this suggestion hears, "You're an idiot for doing it the way you've been doing it—my way is better and I'm smarter than you." This happens because the person's Information Traffic Cop sent the information to the ego instead of the brain. Then the person hearing the new suggestion reacts and says something to the effect "You don't know what you're talking about. You paint people don't know anything about the wheel department. You're the idiots!" Now things are completely out of control. This happens every day, all day.

If you're running the meeting, or if you're in one of the debating groups, you have to reroute the new information away from the egos and to the brains of the people involved and say, "Wait a minute. Hold up. What makes you say you can't put the wheels on it before you paint it? I sincerely want to know, because I'm thinking you have to paint it before you put the wheels on. You're thinking you've got to put the wheels on before you paint it. So tell me why you think that." When you get a logical (not emotional) response and thought process, there could be very good input. Maybe someone's 100% correct, or 100% wrong, but more often than not, the solution lies somewhere in between. The result of the two passionate sides calmly discussing the problem or opportunity will result in a better solution and a more positive result for everyone involved.

The total absence of friction, even Negative Friction, can also point out the absence of opportunity for Positive Friction. What we see in a business environment, or in your personal or family life, is that when someone is vociferously against you it means they care about something passionately. If you find out what that is, then they can become your ally. So the friction is good—it helps you identify who really cares about things.

Dallas Cowboys Coach Bill Parcells said a few players have taken a swing at him in the past . . .

"That's okay. I think confrontation is healthy because it clears the air."

BILL PARCELS

Know your vision, share your vision. You're absolutely nuts if you're working for a company of any size and you're not sharing what you are thinking with everyone around you. This is true 100% of the time–even if whom you're going to talk to might not immediately agree with you about your procedural change, policy adjustment, company goals, etc. Everyone should be open to confrontation, whether you're the employee/underling or the big honcho. Voicing new ideas and opinions is the how people move from the mailroom to the boardroom. Openly encouraging and listening to those different ideas and opinions is how executives get the corner offices.

If someone has a different opinion than yours on virtually any topic and confronts you about it, there are three possible realities:

1.) That person could be completely wrong.
2.) That person could be completely correct.
3.) That person could be partially right.

Unfortunately egos jump out at the first sign of confrontation and assume the first possibility is the reality. If you're the one being confronted with a difference of opinion, recognize that there might be value in what this person has to say. Even if they're only 10% correct, that means a 10% improvement in whatever process, strategy, policy, etc. they're talking about.

A healthy ego isn't afraid of being on either end of a confrontation because, in a controlled ego environment, confrontation should always be very positive.

Confrontation means that two people have a passionate opinion about something. Passionate, controlled confrontation is what leads to better answers, creative solutions and greater success. People with healthy egos aren't timid about expressing their thoughts, but when people are confronted with a different opinion than theirs, whether it comes from an employee, a co-worker, a competitor, a spouse, a parent, a friend, or a supervisor, it's almost always viewed as an assault on their ego. As a result, the other idea, maybe a good one, isn't heard. Explosive egos destroy passion and better ideas are never spoken or considered.

If you're the one who's confronting the other person and presenting the differing opinion, and if you get an initial negative response, use other Friction Factors (i.e.: "Don't Return Fire," "Give 'Em A Cookie," "Correct The Action, Not The Person," etc.) to turn the Negative Friction into Positive Friction. We'll get to those specific Friction Factors shortly, but first things first.

BIG EGO

"The trouble with most of us is that we would rather be ruined by praise than saved by criticism."

DR. NORMAN VINCENT PEALE

Criticism is different than confrontation. As I'm referring to these two concepts, confrontation is a disagreement about a concept, policy, strategy, opinion, etc. Criticism is more about personalities and is more personal in nature. Direct criticism is the easiest way to start an Ego Fire. If you look at quotations on "criticism," you'll find that 99% of people view criticism from one perspective—All criticism is bad and the person doing the criticizing should think twice about doing it. It's all pretty much in the "Judge not lest ye be judged" vein. This couldn't be more wrong.

How often do you become upset when you're criticized? I would answer, "All the time." Your ego is assaulted and Negative Friction is created. To most people, criticism is a negative concept that would then cause Negative Friction. It should be the exact opposite. Criticism is an opportunity to hear another opinion about what you're doing. Even if you initially don't agree with the opinion of the person doing the criticizing, you should still listen for anything that can add value to you, or your concept.

Listen to everything people throw at you, because sometimes even the biggest jerks and the most vicious Ego Monsters have something meaningful to say. They might be saying it for their own vicious, misdirected reasons; but, for you, there might actually be a little something there. So instead of letting your ego take over at the first sign of criticism, you should always listen intently. After listening, never let your ego be wounded (Negative Friction) because somebody criticized you or something you did. You should view the criticism as Positive Friction, but you should be confident enough, smart enough, and have a healthy enough ego to consider the criticism, no matter how harsh.

Criticism can be productive if you always look for valuable morsels. So before you fire the employee who tells you your management style is too abrupt, quit your job because your boss tells you your reports are too vague or do battle with your spouse about putting on a few extra pounds, take a minute to consider the possibility they might actually be right—you could be too abrupt, too vague, or a little too pudgy. Always turn the Negative Friction into Positive Friction.

I seek criticism in my business. Is there a place for someone's ego to seek out criticism? Absolutely. You can ask someone, "How did I do?" It could be a sincere question and you want the feedback, or "How did I do, where's my 'atta boy? I want a compliment." If it's a real question, you'll learn a great deal, grow and succeed. If it's the latter, you're wasting everyone's time.

Albert Einstein once declared that his second greatest idea (after the theory of relativity) was to add an egg while cooking soup in order to produce a soft-boiled egg without having an extra pot to wash.

Friction Factor

2

Beware Of People With No Elbows

"When they discover the center of the universe, a lot of people will be disappointed to discover they are not it."

BERNARD BAILEY

What can't a person do if he or she has no elbows? There are many things, like scratch their nose, button their shirt, brush their teeth, but the most important thing the person with no elbows can't do is point at themselves. Whenever there's a problem all they can do is point at other people. They can't take responsibility for their own actions. In their minds, they can never be wrong. Any challenge or problem is always someone else's fault. When that's the case, their ego is detonated, and negative energy blasts in every direction.

What the No Elbow People don't understand is that it's impossible for anyone to improve themselves or learn anything if they don't make mistakes. No one does everything right all the time. No one!

Your first instinct is probably to ignore these elbow-less people, but you can't do that, at least not forever. These people are in every organization, at every level, and in every area of your life.

If you're dealing with someone who has no elbows, recognize their straight-arm problem and let them know it's okay to make a mistake. Move on, fix it, and create Positive Friction. (We'll deal with the specific Friction Factors of how to manage and control the people with no elbows and their raging egos, but first understand this Friction Factor foundation.)

These elbow-less people can be worker bees or they can be high level executives. They can be a friend, a relative, or a parent on your child's sports team. It could involve a major issue, or something rather small. Something as small as forgetting to send an email to a coworker, or returning a phone call. They just forget to do it, but they don't want anyone to think they messed up and forgot. Therefore, it impacts their ego because they don't want anyone to know they dropped the ball . . . so they just blame it on someone else. "Well, I sent it, didn't you get it? And I left a message." Then the response, "I didn't get an email or a message from you." Now we have two people, and their egos, calling each other a liar . . . that's not where anyone wants to be, and that's not how you create positive energy and a better outcome.

Here's one of the most interesting aspects of the Land of People With No Elbows . . . they don't realize they have no elbows. They think their attitudes and actions are completely correct and justified; that's what makes them so difficult to deal with.

People With No Elbows might be proactive or reactive. Their personalities can take many forms, from loud and violent, to cynical and sarcastic, to calm and arrogant. A No Elbow Ego Monster might be intentionally letting his or her ego attack you, or they might not be aware that the bad ego has come out to play.

Here's another interesting fact, whether you realize it or not, you and your ego have done at least some of the above. If you don't think this is true, that's the first sign of having no elbows.

Consider this, you have a disagreement or conflict with a friend. Privately, each of you would agree that regardless of what the specific facts are, it's obviously an ego-based disagreement, but you'll say that your friend has the ego problem. And your friend will be equally adamant that you're the one who has the inflated ego. That's how virtually everyone on the face of the earth will initially respond—"The problem is the other person's ego." In that common scenario, both you and your friend, and virtually everyone else, have no elbows.

The bottom line is that when No Elbow Ego Monsters take responsibility for their actions, when they say to themselves, "Wait, I'm not a bad person, or stupid, or incompetent because I didn't do this. I just didn't get it done. I just had a bad day" that's when they can grow and that's when they can succeed.

It's okay to be wrong or make a mistake—it happens to everyone. Bend your elbow, point to yourself, and say, "I did it. Sorry" or "My bad." Then move on. Fix it. Create Positive Friction from a negative event.

For example, a customer comes into a furniture store and orders a blue couch. Six weeks later the couch shows up and it's red. The customer wanted a blue couch. Who made the couch red? Who made the mistake? Someone else obviously made and shipped the red couch. The person that sold them the blue couch is the person the customer is dealing with—that's where the friction is. That's where it all starts. Even though that person didn't do anything wrong, it's their responsibility.

Now, the person who's responsible can say to the customer, "Those damn guys down in North Carolina, they made a red couch, I told them it was supposed to be blue. They sent a red one anyway. It's not my fault." There's not an elbow being bent in that situation—and it's the ego responding, not the brain.

The best way to grow that relationship, and keep that customer's business for years to come, is for that person to bend his elbow and say, "You know what, Mr. Smith? I take full responsibility for that. I'm the one that put that order in for the blue couch. I don't know why that red couch came back, but I'm going to make it better. I'm going to fix it, and I will get it taken care of to make sure you're happy."

So many new salespeople want to defend themselves and blame the company. When they bend their elbow, take the blame, and fix the situation, the entire company looks better in the customers' eyes. An elbow was bent, an Ego Flare has been avoided, and that customer will probably be back. Everyone wins.

You want to have elbows, very flexible elbows. How do you make sure you have elbows? You embrace Friction Factor #3. . .

Friction Factor

3

Always Know Where The Finish Line Is

"The lesson that most of us on this voyage never learn, but can never seem to forget, is that to win is sometimes to lose."

RICHARD M. NIXON

"Always Know Where The Finish Line Is" means always know what your end goal is. Somebody says to me," Joel, how do you deal with an Ego Monster?" How do you deal with someone who is just railing at you? Railing at you for no reason. My answer is, "Always Know Where The Finish Line Is." What's the finish line? What do you need to get out of this? Who is this person to you? Will you ever see them again? Do you care who they are? Is this your mother screaming at you? Is this your spouse screaming at you? Is it your child screaming at you? Is it your boss? Is it someone you met on the street? If you have an on-going relationship with this person, a boss, family member or business associate you probably have a goal as simple as keeping your job, getting a promotion or getting along better with your mother-in-law. If it's a spouse the ultimate goal might be to stay married, or have a nice dinner. The point is the long-range goal is what matters, not winning a short-term argument.

Do you have any idea how many people lose a sale, fail to get the account, ruin a negotiation or destroy a relationship, because they lose sight of where the finish line is? The numbers are staggering, and it's all because we lose sight of the real goal. The goal is to make the sale, or get the account, or improve how an office, department, or company is operating, or get along with a friend or family member.

As people become more experienced and accomplished, the more they think they know EVERYTHING about their job; therefore, they must know what's best for their customer, client, employees, or co-workers. Frequently an issue comes up well before the finish line, and they jump out to "win" that disagreement . . . and as a result the sale, account, efficiency, or relationship is lost. They won the argument, but lost the prize. Two examples:

A Client calls his/her Stockbroker and says, "I want to buy some Acme stock." The

Broker says, "I don't recommend that stock." The Client responds, "A guy at the Sushi Bar told me it was about to go up in price, so I want to buy it." The Broker's ego is affected immediately with Negative Friction, and he is now thinking that this Client is an idiot, because of course anyone who wouldn't heed his advice must be stupid. If the ego can be controlled, all will be fine. If not, a relationship can be ruined.

Life Insurance Agents run into the old "term vs. whole life" argument. Again, the Insurance Agent's ego knows all, and therefore, there is no way his client could actually know what he wants—if the ego is allowed to speak for us, potential disaster is at hand.

Why did the Agent argue with them? What was the reason? His ego had to win. But his ego didn't win anything that mattered. The Agent lost.

No one should let another person make an obviously stupid move, but never lose sight of the ultimate goal, and the discussion should be motivated by the mind and heart, not the ego.

A friend once asked me if I ever read Sun Tsu, "The Art of War." At the time I hadn't. He said, "You're like the Sun Tsu warrior—you do all the warrior stuff, you attack when you need to attack, but you don't attack when you shouldn't." That's always knowing where the finish line is, knowing what your ultimate goal is, and not letting your ego prevent you from reaching your goal. "Always Know Where The Finish Line Is." Don't spike the ball at the ten yard line.

This Friction Factor obviously is key with our long term, on-going relationships, but it works equally well with total strangers. Every morning I eat breakfast at the same place. I go in and I sit with the same waitress and I order the same breakfast—I can be a pretty boring guy. Sometimes, I'll get a newspaper on the way in. One morning I walk up to the newspaper machine and I have my coins in my hand all ready to put in the machine for the paper. There's a man standing there, not blocking the machine, not square up to it, sort of at an angle. He's looking at the paper through the glass, and he's kind of looking for change in his pocket, but basically not doing anything, just standing there. Again, not crowding the machine, but a couple of feet away. I have my change ready to go. I stop and I wait. 5 seconds, 10 seconds, 15 seconds. He doesn't really do anything, so I say "excuse me" and I put my money in, I get my paper, and I walk away. This guy starts yelling at me. "Who do you think you are?! You just butt in front of me to get a paper?! Who are you, some big important guy?!" His Information Traffic Cop immediately sent my actions to his ego. I apologize and walk into the diner. I sit at the counter where I always sit and he comes in and he sits two stools down from me and continues to yell. The people behind the counter are watching this scene. I looked at him and said, "I'm sorry. I didn't mean to offend you. You were standing there, I waited. I just got a paper and came inside. I'm sorry." I asked the waitress to move me, and she did. The waitress asked what was going on. "Why was that guy yelling at you? Why didn't you yell back? That guy's a jerk. Do you want us to kick him out?" I thanked her for her concern and support, but told her I didn't know that man and I didn't know if he just separated from his wife, if he was just fired from his job, or if he was just diagnosed with some 'three months to live' disease. I didn't know anything about that guy and why he's in that bad of a mood. I can tell you one thing though, it doesn't have anything to do with me and I don't care . . . I just wanted my paper and my breakfast— that was my finish line, and I got to it.

Another example:

We've all seen this a hundred times. You're checking into a hotel and the guy in front of you wants a room with a king bed. The person at the front desk checks the computer, and there doesn't appear to be any king beds available. The hotel is sold out, but he can have a room with two doubles. Unfortunately, the guy's Information Traffic Cop has messed up and he starts screaming at the clerk at the front desk. "I reserved a king! You told me I was getting a king. I've got my confirmation number right here!" What's the end result this guy wants? Is his goal to scream at a $9 an hour front desk person and make him feel awful? No, he wants a room with a king bed, right? Frequently a king bed can be found even when the computer initially says none are available. Computers have no egos, but people do. Do you think he'll get his king bed by yelling? I don't think so.

All the Friction Factors are important, and they all work in specific situations, but "Always Know Where The Finish Is" is the cornerstone for every potential ego encounter anyone will ever have. If Information Traffic Cops can stay focused on this key Friction Factor, significantly fewer Ego Monsters will emerge.

Toward the end of his life, Thomas Jefferson wrote his own epitaph, and instructed that the inscription contain "not a word more." Accordingly, his epitaph reads: "Here was buried Thomas Jefferson, author of the Declaration of American Independence, of the Statute of Virginia for Religious Freedom, and Father of the University of Virginia."

Incredibly, Jefferson chose not to mention that he was also:

Minister to France (1785–1789)

Secretary of State (1789–1793)

Vice President (1797–1806) and

President of the United States (1802–1809)

4

Don't Return Fire

"Better to give your path to a dog than be bitten by him in contesting for the right. Even killing the dog would not cure the bite."

ABRAHAM LINCOLN

When an ego detonates and explodes in someone's face and verbal missiles are being fired, 98% of people respond in exactly the wrong manner. They say, "Oh yeah? You want to be a jerk to me? Then I'll be a jerk right back at you. Are you going to assault my ego? Fine. I'm going to assault your ego right back." That's normal human instinct, but it's bad human policy.

Examples of this occur with employees and managers, co-workers, spouses, teammates in sports, and parents with their children. It doesn't matter how mad you are, how frustrated you are, or how insane the other person is being—do not react in the same manner in which you're being treated. Never return fire.

"Don't Return Fire" is a tactic to use when an Ego Monster is attacking. When an Ego Monster is being abusive, demeaning, or cruelly sarcastic, the worst thing you can do is lower yourself to his level, respond with anger, and throw more "gas on the flame." If you return fire, you will always create a bigger fire, and more Negative Friction.

We were just dealing with Friction Factor #3, "Always Know Where The Finish Line Is." "Don't Return Fire" is the first rule of keeping your ultimate goal in sight.

When Ego Monster's act this way toward us, all they are really saying is, "Come on, lets go, let's fight! I'm miserable with myself and this situation, so I want you to be miserable too." Misery loves company. The best reaction is no reaction. This might initially make Ego Monsters even more angry, but eventually there is nothing for them to do but calm down.

Instead of returning fire, the first thing you do is inwardly smile. You smile inwardly and realize "I don't know what happened to this guy before I met him, but this Ego Flare (his attitude toward me) certainly has nothing to do with me." The reason you don't smile outwardly at the Ego Monster, is because they'll think you're taunting them, and then you're going to make them twice as mad and twice as out of control. To paraphrase Robert DeNiro's character in the movie Taxi Driver . . . "You Smilin' at me? You smilin' at me? You must be smilin' at me, I'm the only one here." You don't want to do that to the DeNiro character or anyone . . . so smile inwardly.

After your inward smile, you can make sure you're dealing with your brain and not your ego in this situation. Returning Fire will just make a bad situation worse. It will make Negative Friction even more negative. Everyone will lose.

Not firing back at a raving Ego Monster takes a certain degree of self-control. Why is that? We want to respond because it's our nature to not want to lose—not even this one argument or confrontation with this out of control Ego Monster. If we lose an argument, we think that's bad. If we lose face, we think that's bad. If the other person wins, we think that's bad. We're programmed that way. Who made the better point? Who got the last word?

So, because we're programmed to want to win every time, if we don't respond to the Ego Monster's verbal attack, stop arguing, and say nothing, it appears that we lost. The Ego Monster must have been right because we didn't refute anything he said, we backed down—so they won and we lost. Wrong! That might be how some will interpret the situation, but they couldn't be more wrong.

When you "Don't Return Fire," you win. You win because you realized what was going on in this "conversation" and you win by refusing to lower yourself to a mindless verbal confrontation. You maintained your dignity, didn't turn Negative Friction into a roaring fire that could've done even more damage to everyone involved, and your ultimate goal (your Finish Line) is still achievable.

Some might say by not returning fire you swallowed your pride. I don't agree. By not returning fire you realized what the real situation was and you responded intelligently and wisely. Not only did you not swallow your pride, but by not returning fire, you're the only one who has a right to be proud.

"Don't Return Fire" is something you should obviously do when you are face to face with an Ego Monster. But there's another, less obvious, much more subtle Ego Trap where you should take a deep breath and smile inwardly, twice—you can even smile outwardly in this particular situation. It's when an Ego Monster unleashes his rage in an email or voice mail bomb. Be very careful with letters, emails and voice mail. You're not face-to-face with the Ego Monster, so it's remarkably easy to lose sight of your finish line and ultimate goal, and return fire. Think, smile, think again before you put words to paper, fingers to keys or mouth to the phone. Make sure your brain is typing or talking and not your ego.

"Don't Return Fire" is the most important first step to calming a raging ego and starting to turn Negative Friction into Positive Friction, but is there any action you can take to improve the situation and calm the Ego Monster? Yes, you move to Friction Factor #5 . . .

Beatles drummer Ringo Starr was once asked the secret of the band's success. Ringo's reply? "We have a press agent."

5

Give 'Em A Cookie

"I can live for two months on one good compliment."

MARK TWAIN

As we've already discussed, never return fire. So what can you do when face to face with an Ego Monster who's growling, snarling, and barking at you? You do the same thing that you'd do if faced with a growling, snarling, barking Doberman . . . you "Give 'Em A Cookie." A Cookie, in this case, is a compliment, a statement of agreement, or some satisfaction aimed at whatever it is that is causing the Negative Friction.

Cookie is a metaphor for compliment or something that will put some balm on the burn. Basically, when somebody is raging at you, they're usually not raging at you. They're raging in general and you just happened to be in the way. Most people react by raging back. We already know not to do that. "Don't Return Fire." There's more than just not raging back.

For instance: You're being berated by an Ego Monster supervisor because your department is behind schedule for meeting your quarterly goal. Remember, the finish line is to meet the goal by the end of the quarter, not win this particular argument. So what might happen if you said, "You're right. We are behind schedule. You've had a lot of experience at this. Help me, what can we do differently to meet the quarterly goal?" Instantly, you can turn Negative Friction into Positive Friction.

Also, realize that a Cookie is a genuine compliment or positive statement. Insincere and shallow flattery won't work. For instance . . . "That's a great looking toupee, boss. Is it new?" probably won't get your desired result. "Give 'Em A Cookie" doesn't mean being a kiss-up.

Deflect and address the situation. Giving an Ego Monster a Cookie usually puts out the fire very quickly. Most of us are offended by an Ego Monster's behavior, then we get mad, then we treat the monster the same way he is treating us. What does that solve? Nothing. Be a bigger person. "Give 'Em A Cookie." In fact, give the Monster as many Cookies as it takes to create Positive Friction, therefore, creating a positive result.

Another example: Coaching little league, youth soccer, peewee football, etc... It's not uncommon for parents standing on the sidelines to be screaming at the coaches. I continue to find this parental conduct a complete mystery, but we're not here to cure bizarre behavior, we just want to know how to deal with these people. So, what do you do with a parent gone nuts? Do you ignore it? Do you address it? How do you get them to calm down? Usually, what I do is involve them. I give them a Cookie. I say to them, "You seem upset about what's going on. Tell me, what am I not doing here? Help me out. What would you do? I sincerely want to know. I'd like to learn." That Cookie pacifies just about any maniac out there.

Remember our Ego Monster buddy getting his morning paper? The Cookie that I gave him was, I said, "I didn't mean to offend you. I'm sorry if I did anything wrong" and I left. Now, most people would not say they're sorry for that. Why would they? They didn't do anything wrong.

They don't need to apologize, right? This guy is a maniac, an Ego Monster. Why should they apologize to a maniac? I say, "Who cares?" I didn't return fire, I gave him a Cookie, and he went away. No harm, no foul. I certainly don't feel like he won and I lost. I don't care. I read my paper, ate my breakfast and got on with my day. I heard a relationship expert say the most important thing to a woman is not the quality of the gift, but the quantity of gifts. He said one rose a day for 12 days is a thousand times better than a dozen roses at one time. Little notes, voicemails, acknowledgments, which are actually little Cookies, can diffuse an Ego Monster or help build good will and possibly avoid a potential Ego Fire.

At work, a Cookie can be involvement in a project the worker normally wouldn't be involved in. Maybe something unique that's going on with the office or business. Something to make them feel better about themselves to calm that rage a little bit or prevent any rage from occurring. Acknowledgment and involvement are two areas that qualify as Cookies—and they can be given before, during, or after an Ego Flare.

If a person tends to have a negatively impacted ego due to her own self esteem issues then she needs to be involved. Giving that person a Cookie might be calling her and asking her advice on something. You might not think you need that person's advice, but she feels good giving it to you—and, who knows, you might get some very good input if you let the advice go directly to your brain. That's one of the best Cookies you can give people—asking for their advice and their involvement.

When you give an Ego Monster a Cookie, you're swallowing your pride even though maybe you wanted to hit the Ego Monster over the head with the nearest heavy object. You're saying, "Here you go buddy, have a Cookie." A Cookie helps calm a raging ego and helps you get to your finish line and your ultimate goal.

BIG EGO

"Benjamin Franklin devised a week-by-week plan to improve his character by working on thirteen virtues. Franklin's sharp focus, meticulous record-keeping, and diligent work yielded improvements in the first twelve virtues—temperance, silence, order, resolution, frugality, industry, sincerity, justice, moderation, tranquility, cleanliness and chastity. However, he found that every time he began to make progress in developing humility, he got proud of it!"

We Interrupt This Book For An Important Announcement

Some of you might have seen this coming, some of you haven't. Some of you will accept this fact, others will fight it—but it's 100% true, and it's the single most important element in turning Negative Friction into Positive Friction and controlling the Ego Monsters.

We've been talking about out of control Ego Monsters. Virtually everyone reading this book has one ego in mind, one ego that's at fault, one ego that's out of control, one ego that needs fixing . . . and that ego is the other guy's ego. I'm sure the other person, or people, you have in mind is an Ego Monster that needs controlling, but the most important ego for you to deal with, manage, and control to avoid an Ego Explosion is YOUR own ego.

"MY EGO? NO WAY! THE PROBLEM IS HIS EGO!"

Yes, the other guy probably is the problem, no argument there. BUT . . . Anytime there's friction between two people, it takes both people to turn the friction into an Ego Fire. Only one person, YOU, can control your own ego and turn that Negative Friction into Positive Friction to calm the situation and prevent an Ego Fire from igniting. When you control and manage your ego, you can control and manage other egos . . . then you control your world.

At the critical moment, no one ever realizes that their Information Traffic Cop has sent a statement to their ego. Everyone, even the worst Ego Monsters in the middle of a massive Ego Explosion, are sure they're using their logical brain and not their emotional ego. Unless you concentrate and focus on the Friction Factors and consciously turn Negative Friction into Positive Friction, you'll probably make the same mistake more often than you realize.

Some of the first five Friction Factors do deal directly with you and your ego, but all the Friction Factors run through your ego. Reread the first five Friction Factors, but this time read them with YOUR ego in mind, and not just the other Ego Monster.

"Don't Return Fire" is all about you and your ego. So is "Give 'Em A Cookie." "Beware Of People With No Elbows" is dead-on when it comes to the Ego Monsters in your life—but ask yourself, do you always have elbows? Again, reread the first five Friction Factors with you and your Information Traffic Cop in mind.

These Friction Factors make sense and they work, but now we come to the second step—reading the Friction Factors and understanding them is step one. Step two is making them work in your daily life.

Let's be honest. Actually being able to control yourself to the point where you're not stooping to the Ego Monster's level isn't an easy thing for most of us to do, at least not in the beginning. "Don't Return Fire" is obviously the smart course of action, or inaction, but when some jerk is in your face, it's hard not to respond in kind . . . but you shouldn't. To not fire back is difficult, but to then "Give 'Em A Cookie" could be the single most difficult thing to do in life, maybe with the exception of childbirth. You can, however, make using the Friction Factors not only easy, but your natural way of thinking.

The reality is there are going to be people in your life every single day who are going to be Ego Monsters and create Ego Flares and Ego Fires. The big problem is you usually don't see an Ego Explosion coming until you're right in the middle of it. As a result, you're caught off guard, you're unprepared, and your ego instantly gets involved and responds in the wrong way—which only makes the situation worse.

The thing you have to do, and you can easily do this, is to first recognize when you're in an Ego Situation. Recognize you're facing an Ego Flare or Ego Monster. When you recognize the situation you're in and realize what's happening, your Information Traffic Cop can calmly and thoughtfully send all the incoming statements and actions to your brain, not your ego.

As I've said, putting some or all the Friction Factors to work isn't necessarily the easiest path to take, but if your brain is in charge, your brain can create the discipline you need to not lower yourself to the Ego Monster's level. Always keep Friction Factor #3 in focus—"Always Know Where The Finish Line Is." Winning is important, but winning an insignificant skirmish and losing the big prize is not winning—it's losing. Egos have no discipline, just raw emotion. Being disciplined, using your mind, and staying above the Ego Fray allows you to control and manage the Ego Monsters and helps you attain your ultimate goal. Discipline allows you to turn Negative Friction into Positive Friction.

The next five Friction Factors are aimed directly at you and your ego. These five Friction Factors, and all the Friction Factors, enable you to control your Information Traffic Cop and your ego so you can ultimately manage and control Ego Flares, Ego Fires, Ego Explosions, and Ego Monsters.

Friction Factor

6

One Up Is Really One Down

"Maturity begins to grow when you can sense your concern for others outweighing your concern for yourself."

JOHN MACNAUGHTON

Someone says, "I just got a new car. It's great. It has 350 horsepower and it's the fastest car around, but it still gets 30 miles per gallon!" The other person then says, "Last week I got a new car too, and it has 400 horsepower and gets 40 miles per gallon."

Or it could be even smaller. You say to your friend, "Hey, check out my new cell phone. It makes calls, takes pictures, tells me if the produce is fresh, and whether my kids are lying to me. Is this thing cool or what?" You're happy about it. And your friend says, "I just got the newer one. It has twice as many features—and it automatically calls my psychiatrist when it feels I'm depressed. It's even cooler."

This is classic one-upsmanship. Why? For some reason we feel assaulted when hearing about something the other person has gained, purchased, accomplished, etc. If parents are happy because their son was just accepted to Ed & Ned's College of Taxidermy, why does an Ego Monster have to immediately point out that their kid's at Princeton? They have to make sure that the other guy knows they have something better. Why? What good came of it? The Ego Monster one-upped a co-worker/employee/boss/friend and now that person feels bad . . . and probably annoyed, if not mad.

You might not even realize what you're doing. It could be unconsciously done. You probably didn't mean to, but you created Negative Friction. "One Up Is Really One Down."

Another, possibly well meaning remark, but ultimately one-upping: Let's say someone just bought an item or product that, for whatever reason, wasn't a good buy and you know it. If this person is in the process of buying it, obviously you should tell them what you know before they make the purchase, but if this person already bought the car/tv/vacation whatever, why say anything negative? Why make them feel bad? People do it all the time. "Oh, you bought that car? You should've told me. I know a leasing agent, he could have gotten you a better car at the same price." All that person is doing is hurting the other person, directly attacking their ego, and creating Negative Friction. They're not only one-upping the person after the fact, but also putting them down, and now the person feels like they have to one-up you back. Nothing good is going to come from that.

If you're the victim of one-upsmanship don't make their negative energy worse. Remember, if you do get one-upped— "Don't Return Fire" and "Always Know Where The Finish Line Is."

Another example:

A person hears "I'm really excited. I just got a promotion at work." That statement can go to the Information Traffic Cop, be sent right to the ego, and become Negative Friction. This is because what the person heard was, "Look how good I am, and what a loser you are." Is that what was actually said? Of course not, but that's what the ego heard, and Negative Friction occurred.

When somebody tells you they did something good, how do you fight the urge to go back and top them? You have to take a step back. You have to take a breath and you have to listen to what is going on and you have to say to yourself, "Why do I feel the need to one-up this person? Why do I care? His success doesn't hurt me. Good for that guy."

If you care about the person, you should be happy for them. Even if you don't like them, it does absolutely no good, and it accomplishes absolutely nothing in the long run, to one-up the person. There's never a time when one-upping is good. Ever.

Be confident in yourself and who you are. No one is attacking you, or making a judgment about you when they share a success story with you. Even if they are, don't worry about it. You have your own goals to focus on.

BE PROUD NOT COMPETITIVE & GIVE CREDIT

Instead of One-Upping someone, do the opposite—Be Proud, Not Competitive. Don't be afraid to give others credit for an idea, solution or work well done. It will massively pay off for you and everyone involved.

One of the biggest obstacles to success in business and life is our inability to give credit when credit is due. Our egos often say, "Don't praise that person, because then it will make them look smarter/ more successful/better than you." The other all-too-common-thought is, "They would never have gotten there without me. I'm the only reason they're even successful." Okay, so what? Maybe it's half true or all true—it doesn't matter. Don't be competitive with someone else's success or achievements. Negative Friction is created by this behavior. Be proud. If one of your friends or employees has a significant achievement in their life, be proud of them, be supportive of them, give them credit for what they've accomplished. Don't immediately compete with their achievement just to make you and your ego feel good.

I can't begin to tell you how many times I've seen a boss take an employee's great idea and make it their own, without ever giving any credit to the person that conceived the idea. It happens every day, in just about every company in the world. Why? The boss's ego says, "Uh oh, if everyone finds out how smart/creative that person is, then I won't have a job anymore." Negative Friction. How does the person with the great idea feel? Do you think they'll be so quick to get involved next time? Businesses suffer immensely from this type of activity.

Your job is to help everyone around you achieve his or her goals and dreams, and then you'll always get what you want. When the Ego Monster comes out, everyone loses.

Friction Factor

7

Correct The Action, Not The Person

"Kindness is the oil that takes the friction
out of life."

ANONYMOUS

Smart people, on occasion, do stupid things—it happens. Stupid people do stupid things more often, but neither group wants to be told they're stupid. It's the ego that tells someone he or she is stupid, not the mind and heart.

In college I took a class called Early Childhood Development. That class affected me more than any other class I ever took. I learned that when a child does something bad, you don't say, "You're a bad kid." You say, "What you did was wrong, but you're a good kid." I realized that approach works on everyone from 3 to 93. (People over 93 tend to have totally controlled their egos and don't care what anyone says to them.)

If an Ego Monster tells someone they're a moron because they didn't do an assignment correctly, they'll crush (create Negative Friction) that person's ego real fast. The object wasn't to smash an ego but to get the assignment done correctly. Maybe that person didn't understand the instructions, or received the wrong instructions. Or maybe they just got it wrong—that happens to all of us. When an ego is crushed, that ego has to be put back in shape again if that person is going to do his or her best work. If you want the situation and that person's work to improve, then you must turn potentially Negative Friction into Positive Friction. The Ego Monster would say, "Nice work, mud-for-brains. You're now officially the dumbest human being on the planet." What should be said is "This shouldn't have happened. Let's make sure it doesn't happen again."

If you're the target of the remark, again, realize you're dealing with an Ego Monster. Don't make the situation worse. "Don't Return Fire." You can ask for clarity, or "Give 'Em A Cookie" and ask for their advice on how to do a better job the next time.

In the mortgage business, the biggest mistake loan officers make is telling a customer they will get a certain interest rate before being actually able to lock the rate in to a specific product. The customer then assumes they are getting a specific rate and, when they can't have that rate, they become very upset. The loan officer promised the customer that rate. As the business owner, I'm responsible for making it right with the customer. Honoring the loan officer's mistake might cost me $5,000.00 to satisfy the customer. What do I say to the employee? Well, the bottom line is typically when those things happen, it's a rookie mistake and it's not that the employee is a bad person, or even bad at their job, it's just that the situation got out of control and the loan officer didn't know how to handle it and didn't bring it to me up front. I sit down with them and explain how to not put themselves in that situation ever again. I don't say they were a bad salesperson or a bad loan officer. What they did was bad and here's why. What they did was wrong and here's why. Here's why and how not to do what you just did.

When you tell them this, they feel pain. The boss is telling them they made a mistake. There's a certain amount of friction that has to be there for them to follow directions, but it has to be Positive Friction. Something has to grow out of this. One of the things I'll do is have them write down everything they learned. Having them write down everything they learned as opposed to everything they did wrong creates Positive Friction.

One of the most frustrating things my kids have ever done is very common. They wrote on the walls. When you first see it, you want to yell, but you know you can't. I sit down with my kids and I explain why they can't write on the wall and why it's wrong to write on the wall. Not that they're bad. With kids, you need to reassure them. It's the same with employees, co-workers, friends, spouses, and parents. Everyone needs to be reassured one time or another. If, however, someone's doing something deliberately wrong, and they know that your reaction will be negative, then they have the ego problem. That requires a different approach and a sincere heart-to-heart talk. If a 14 year old writes on the wall, that's a deliberate action. In that case you might have a problem that isn't going to be solved in this book.

Friction Factor

8

Kill The But Man

"He who is good at making excuses is seldom good for anything else."

BENJAMIN FRANKLIN

Everyone has a little person deep inside of them called the But Man. The Information Traffic Cop works right on the surface, the But Man is deeper down and resides with your ego. This little person's job is to protect your ego or, in other words, to "protect your dignity." Ideally, you want your Information Traffic Cop to send everything to your brain, not your ego, but that doesn't always happen.

The But Man stops us from learning, growing, and succeeding. The But Man is the person in charge of creating the excuses for why we are who we are, or why we didn't do something, or why we didn't do our homework, or why we don't have a million dollars.

One of your co-workers gets promoted to the job that you wanted and you immediately think, "Oh, I could've had that job if I wanted it, *but* I had some personal issues outside of work that held me back." Or "I could've been promoted, *but* I didn't kiss up to the boss like that other guy did." The But Man quickly steps in to make you feel better. The But Man is always ready with a great excuse for why you don't have what you want or why you're not where you want to be.

When you "Kill The But Man," it releases you to do anything you want, be anyone you want to be, have anything you want. When the But Man is gone, anything is possible. Another bonus . . .When you "Kill The But Man," your elbows will immediately be able to bend.

An example:

Your boss says, "What's happening with the Smith account?" If you have bad news about the Smith account, the But Man is immediately awakened from his slumber—he's on call 24/7. As soon as he detects incoming fire or notices a blip on the radar, he's at attention immediately and he steps right in front—"Oh no, you're not going to hurt our ego. No, no, no, not our ego." The But Man is the guardian of the ego. So in comes the boss, or spouse, or friend, whoever it is, and they are questioning how you handled something. Maybe you're thinking, "She probably thinks I'm an idiot. She must think I'm an idiot. If she's questioning me, she must think I'm an idiot." So the But Man says, "You're not calling us an idiot." Then at the But Man's urging, you say, "I would have done that, but I didn't because (excuse goes here)." The But Man just takes over and does his job, but your elbows didn't bend and you're approaching this situation with your ego, not your brain. As a result, the odds of something good, Positive Friction, coming out of this situation are fast approaching zero.

When you let the But Man start "butting" immediately, you're not listening. You don't hear what the person is saying. You're just giving excuses immediately and not listening, hearing, or learning. Your mouth is open and your elbows won't bend . . . bad stuff is on the way.

When you "Kill The But Man" there's nobody left to protect your ego. So you're forced to think about whatever is confronting you. When you "Kill The But

Man," there's nobody there to automatically give you the excuse. It's not coming out of your mouth right away. You can take a breath and think a minute—think about what's going on for a moment, and get the information to your brain instead of the But Man and your ego. "Did I really do that, or did I not do that?" You don't want to admit to something you honestly didn't do, but you have to listen, hear, and think before you speak.

The But Man is ALL about ego. It's your ego that causes you to make those excuses. In the person's mind, they need the But Man to protect their fragile ego. They need the But Man to protect their feelings. The But Man is essentially a liar, he makes you feel good, he let's you off the hook, he gives you a defense for whatever challenge you are facing. The But Man is there to make sure that you can always justify your actions to your ego, so you'll feel good. When your ego is assaulted with Negative Friction, you can combat it with Positive Friction to solve the problem/challenge (example, admitting your mistake or shortcoming) or you can react with Negative Friction, an excuse, or a combative answer.

Example: You're in a meeting. It's your turn to present an idea, and you do. You really haven't thought it through, you just throw it out there. One of your co-workers says, "That idea doesn't make any sense. I don't see how it could work." You immediately go into defensive mode. You respond with a barrage of reasons why the idea will work, even though you now realize that your idea maybe wasn't so hot. The But Man has clearly taken over. He's protecting your ego from being hurt. We all hate to be wrong. Our immediate reaction to our co-worker was . . . "I'm right, you are wrong, and I'll prove it." That's the But Man talking. The Positive Friction reaction is, "Hmmm, what makes you say that? I must be missing something. Explain to me why you feel my idea won't work." Then shut up and listen. If you're wrong, admit it. It's okay. It doesn't mean you're stupid, just because you are wrong.

There's a huge difference between excuses and the real reason that something didn't happen. There can be a legitimate reason, but you should know what the reason is. What's the real reason? Is it because you just didn't do it? Not "The dog ate my homework." You never did your homework. That's the real reason. That's fine, but know that's what happened. You just didn't do it—correct the action and move forward and be better next time.

Killing your But Man will allow you to embrace Friction Factor #9—"The A Line"......

Friction Factor

9

The A Line.
Admit. Ask. Adjust. Achieve.

*"Every man I meet is in some way my superior,
and I can learn from him."*

RALPH WALDO EMERSON

One of the biggest life changing events for me was when I learned to ask questions when I didn't understand what was being said to me. At the same time, I also learned how to remove my paradigms about a new idea or concept by only allowing Positive Friction to enter my thought process. No more sitting in a business meeting or having a casual conversation with a co-worker, employee, or friend, and mindlessly nodding my head or, even worse, mentally checking out of the conversation because I "thought" I knew what was going on. I know this sounds basic and very obvious. In reality, when confronted with a situation or challenge that we don't understand or agree with, it is commonplace to nod our heads and pretend like we understand. Why do we do this? We do it because we think we'll look stupid or unintelligent if we don't immediately understand or "get" what is being communicated to us. Our ego says, "Stand there and look like you know what is going on, and that way we'll look just as smart as everyone else."

Can you imagine going through life nodding your head like you know everything? Well, that's what a lot of us do. If you are sitting in a meeting with 15 of your co-workers and your boss/peer/co-worker is explaining a new idea/change/protocol and you don't understand what they're talking about, engage your brain, not your ego. Raise your hand and say, "Excuse me, but I don't have any idea what you're talking about. Can you please explain that again, so I get it? It's really important that I understand, so we can accomplish this new idea/change/protocol as effectively as possible." Then, quickly look around the room and notice how many other people are REALLY glad and RELIEVED that you asked for clarification. It happens every time. If you don't "get it", there is a high probability that there are others that don't "get it" either. Imagine the Positive Friction in a meeting, when everyone truly "gets it" and can contribute their ideas to make the new idea/change/protocol even better. We CANNOT live our whole lives pretending we know everything, just because we think others will judge us as "stupid". When you start asking questions, you become the smartest person in the room, immediately.

Admit—Admit to yourself that you don't understand

Ask—Ask for clarification when you don't "get it"

Adjust—Adjust your thought process to accept and understand the new idea or concept

Achieve—Achieve incredible growth by learning something new or embracing a new concept

Initially, this is a tough obstacle for anyone, but once you accept this seemingly contrary strategy, you're on the fast track to success.

You will radically change your life when you ignore your ego and start to ask questions when you don't understand what's being said to you. At the same time, you'll also learn how to remove obstacles to a new idea or concept by allowing Positive Friction to enter your thought process.

I had a boss who used a wonderful phrase to make sure he understood what people wanted him to know. He'd say, "Do me a favor. Give it to me in the kindergartner version, because I have no idea what you're talking about." Adjust, which is adjust your thinking, and achieve. Every single time.

A true, life changing story:

Many years ago I became the youngest Branch Manager for a big company. The company made me a manager when I was only in my mid-twenties. I was significantly younger than most of the other managers in this company. Within the first couple of months, there was an important manager's meeting. Managers and their supervisors from the whole company were there. I sat at the back of the room and listened intently to all the information and presentations. I was a rookie manager and I was taking a lot of notes. The last speaker before lunch was the Chairman and President of the company. I was in the last row, my immediate boss was closer to the front. The President started to speak, and he went on about loan profitability and ROI, yadda-yadda-yadda. I had no idea what he was talking about. Then he broke out the graphs and slides, but what he was talking about didn't get any clearer. So I raised my hand—"Excuse me." My boss, and pretty much everyone else there, looked at me with absolute horror. "This kid is interrupting the king!" It's like stopping the Pope during a service. But I kept at it until the President saw me. He said, "Yes?" I said, "I hope you don't take this wrong, but I have no idea what you're talking about. Can you go over that again, because I know what you're talking about effects me, but I just don't get it." It's a cliché, but you could've heard a pin drop. . .and the room was carpeted. The 40 and 50 year old career managers, with their white starched shirts and red banker ties were intently watching for the President's reaction. The President was thinking about what I had just said, wheels were turning. Then he said to me, "Sure. What don't you understand?" I asked what in hindsight was a simple question about ROI, which he answered. Then I asked a couple other questions, which the President gladly answered. "Okay. You got it now?" I said I did, and thanked him. He resumed his presentation. When he finished, it was time to break for lunch. The President walked from the front of the room; and, of course, he was mobbed by all the sycophants who wanted to talk to him. He broke through the crowd, came to the back of the room, grabbed me and took me out in the hall to talk to me about my questions and focus—I was actually listening and he knew that.

That was the beginning of a beautiful relationship. Everybody in that room was scared to death to look like an idiot, except me. Fortunately, I was just too dumb to realize that I shouldn't ask any "stupid" questions.

Several months after assuming my new position as a manager, people in the office were resigning in droves. This was very upsetting to me and I thought I wasn't doing my job correctly. The President called me. He said, "I just wanted to tell you that I know you're up there by yourself, and I totally support you. I want you to make that YOUR office. Hire all new people. I know you're going to be successful." . . . and, I say, with modesty, I was. Much of what I achieved can be directly traced back to the time I admitted I didn't understand what was being said, asked a few questions, and adjusted my thinking.

I tell my kids this story (probably too often in their opinion). It's never too early to adopt "The A Line." How many kids just sit in class and let knowledge and education go by because they don't want to raise their hand. They should ask the question. It's an important question, ask it. If you don't know, others probably don't know either.

Same example, different angle: Think about the previous example not from my perspective, but instead from the President/speaker's point of view. When you're the one making the presentation, don't let your ego cause you to be less effective than you want to be, and can be. It's not about the speaker, it's about the audience. It's not what you give them, it's what they get. You have to care about who you're talking to. You have to worry about their egos. Make sure they're going to understand. You already get it. You don't have to play some game. Here's what we're doing, blah blah blah. See how smart I am? Not everyone will have read this book, so not everyone will admit they don't get it, and ask you to clarify. The President could've had an ego reaction to my interrupting him, and my life might've been different. But he didn't— his Information Traffic Cop sent my question to his brain.

If you're the boss, and everyone is the boss of something or someone, keep the egos of those you interact with healthy and strong. Short-circuit their But Men. Encourage them to ask questions if they don't understand. Make sure your ego is healthy enough not to take offense if someone asks you a question. A question doesn't mean that you're an idiot, it just means you need to explain the issue in a different way. Your Information Traffic Cop should direct a question to your brain, not your ego.

One day during the production of *The Replacements*, Keanu Reeves requested that his trailer be replaced with another model. The problem? His trailer was too large and extravagant. He wanted something smaller, in deference to the rest of the cast.

Friction Factor

10

The E Triangle

"The greatest genius will not be worth much if he pretends to draw exclusively from his own resources."

JOHANN WOLFGANG VON GOETHE

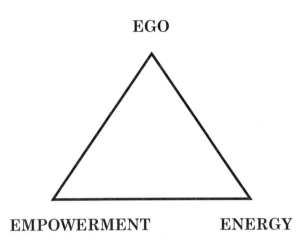

EGO

EMPOWERMENT ENERGY

To tie together all the Friction Factors, concepts and strategies in this book, you must understand the importance of "The E Triangle." "The E Triangle" consists of Ego, Empowerment, and Energy. These three E's are universally connected together to affect everything you do and say.

If your Ego is so out of control that you think you know everything, you'll never Empower the people around you. If you don't have Empowered people, nothing happens unless you do it yourself, and the only energy used and created is your own

Negative Friction. When the Energy is removed from any situation, very little is accomplished. This is true with employees, associates, family and friends.

If your Ego is healthy, you'll Empower those around you to do what they need to do, which in turn creates a huge amount of Energy, which creates Positive Friction. Empowered people are always successful people, and if everyone around you is successful, then chances are, you will be successful too. Understanding how these three E's are interconnected is crucial to being successful in business, as a parent, as a friend and, of course, as a person.

Ego, Empowerment, and Energy equal strength. Strength equals success. You have to empower in order for there to be energy for things to get done, achievements realized, and goals to be met. There are offices and businesses all over the world where productivity is a fraction of what it should be because the boss basically never lets anybody do anything, and never shows anybody how to do anything. These bosses run their offices or companies with Negative Friction. They run the office, department or business based on how their ego is impacted, and the resulting Negative Friction. These people don't want to let anyone do anything because, God forbid, what if someone would do something better than they do? These bosses, specifically their egos, won't empower anyone to do anything. As a result, the energy in that operation is very low, if it exists at all.

When people are empowered, that creates energy. If there's no empowerment, there's no energy, and basically nothing ever gets done.

An ego is a wonderful thing. A healthy ego results in productive self-confidence. With self-confidence, different opinions can be considered and correct decisions made. Success is realized, goals are met, and dreams come true because people have healthy egos and self-confidence. Successful business leaders and leaders in all areas of society have healthy egos and believe they can get things done—so they do.

If your ego is not operating with Positive Friction, then you never empower anyone to do anything. Your ego has to be positive. Yes, you have to use your brain more often than your ego, but everyone has an ego and that ego has to be healthy and secure. It has to create Positive Friction to be able to empower and to be able to create energy.

There are many people, not just bosses, but coworkers, family members and friends, who refuse to empower the people around them for fear those people will outshine them. That, all too often, is the story of corporate America. That's people complaining about their boss—"I never get a chance" or "He never lets me do it" or "He never shows me how to do it." When people go into their boss's office with a problem, he or she says, "I'll fix it" instead of "Here's how you fix it." In an environment of "I'll fix it" this translates to "I know what I'm doing, you don't," "I'm smart, you're dumb," no one is empowered, and no energy is or can be created. That is always a low production office, filled will unhappy, unproductive workers. That's always true. That manager, that leader, that vice president, no matter how talented or brilliant, can only do so much in one day.

Mac Brown, the football coach at the University of Texas is a man who understands "The E Triangle." Coach Brown was asked about his former star quarterback, Vince Young. There was a huge difference between Texas quarterback Vince Young as a freshman and Vince Young the quarterback on the Rose Bowl winning, National Championship team just a couple of years later. When asked what he did to cause such improvement in the talented athlete, Brown had a simple answer, he said he finally learned to just let Vince be Vince, and create an environment where Vince could be successful. When that happened, Vince exploded into a superstar and everyone benefited. This is "The E Triangle" at work.

An example of "The E Triangle" from my own childhood:

When I was in elementary school, I received an allowance. My dad said, "Okay, lunch is 80 cents every day. You get $5 a week. You can buy your lunch everyday, and you have a dollar left over. If you spend it all, then you have to make your lunch and take it yourself." I was empowered when I was a child, and it made an impression. It didn't stop there. All through my life I was empowered like that. When I turned 16, my dad said to me, "If you want more money, go get a job. And by the way, if you get a job, I'll give you an allowance. If you don't get a job, I won't." So I got a job, and an allowance. You might consider this parental logic counterintuitive, but it's not. My parents rewarded the responsible behavior. I was empowered. I was fueled with positive energy to be a successful person.

As a result, when I went to college, I was very responsible. I could earn a certain amount of money monthly, and be fine with it. I never ran out of cash before the end of the month. I didn't have any credit cards. I was on my own. I met people in college who were calling their parents when they were 20 years old, to ask for $50. These were the kids who when they were in high school and wanted to go to the movies, would go to their parents and say, "I want to go to the movies. Can I have $20." When I was in high school, if I wanted to go to a movie, I went to a movie. If I didn't have the money, I didn't go. I wasn't going to go ask for money again, because I already had it. It was allowance. If I spent it, I spent it.

Mothers and Fathers who I call "under my thumb parents" are parents whose egos are out of control. These are parents who want to completely control their children. They never empower their kids, and probably don't empower the people who work for and with them either. I strongly believe the children of the "under my thumb parents" have a much harder time succeeding as adults. The only way they're successful is if they go into their parent's business and they're controlled for the rest of their life until their parents die. I have rarely met one kid who was brought up in that environment who became a successful adult. This wasn't meant to be a diatribe on good parenting, merely the importance of "The E Triangle" and the parallels to virtually every area of life.

The first thing I try to teach managers and supervisors to do is get out of your own way. Take a minute and find out what all your people want. What does the person in front of you really want, really need? Once you can figure that out, it's your job as the dynamic leader, manager, owner, friend, spouse or parent to figure out how that person's goal and agenda can become part of your goal and agenda. Guess what . . . Sometimes it's not. When it's not, people that work with me tend to quit. Fortunately, that's a very infrequent situation. Healthy egos can empower others, and help make those other egos healthy.

BIG EGO

When you let someone know that you're there for them, that you honestly care about the fact that their ego is healthy, this knowledge affects their thoughts, their ideas, their goals, and what they want. They become empowered, significantly more energized, and massively more productive.

Philip II (the father of Alexander the Great) employed two men whose sole responsibility was to address him twice each day. Their morning duty? To say: "Philip, remember that you are but a man." And in the evening? To ask: "Philip, have you remembered that you are but a man?"

Final Thought

These ten Friction Factors will work for you in more ways than you can imagine. Keep this book close by and when you see an Ego Flare, or read about an Ego Monster, or hear about an Ego Explosion, read through this book again. The longer you deal with the Friction Factors, and the more you observe people letting their Information Traffic Cop send information to their ego instead of their brains, the better you'll become at controlling and managing all the egos around you.

BUT . . . there's one last ego reality I want you to understand. I don't care how well you use the Friction Factors, or how in control you are of your own ego and the Ego Monsters in your life, there are times when the Friction Factors aren't going to be as effective as they can be, at least not at that particular moment. Sometime you'll be faced with an Ego Monster and absolutely nothing you can say or do will get this lunatic to stop thinking with her ego and use her brain. Nothing you can do at the time can turn this Negative Friction into Positive Friction. In those instances, do what your brain is telling you to do . . . disengage. You extricate yourself from the Ego Monster and the Ego Explosion. Sometimes you just have to walk away, not storm out and slam doors as you leave, but realize that no Positive Friction can possibly be created in this irrational environment, and as politely as possible end the conversation.

If it's a boss, co-worker, friend or family member, you may simply agree to disagree for the moment. If it's a total stranger, just walking away might be the best course of action. Again, always keep Friction Factor #3 in clear focus— "Always Know Where The Finish Line Is." Sometimes the wisest action to take to gain your important long-term goal is to retreat. You may not feel good about backing down, but you haven't done any damage, and your ultimate goal is still attainable.

Later you can go back when emotions have calmed down. Hopefully, the Ego Monster is using her brain now instead of her ego, but in any event the situation should be less heated. You can re-engage the topic, whatever it was, and calmer, less emotional heads will prevail.

Sometimes there's no reason to even try to resolve an ego-based conflict because, at that moment, nothing will turn Negative Friction into Positive Friction. Nothing will soothe or slay the Ego Monster. I'm sure there are times when both husbands and wives feel like their spouse has jumped into a foxhole with a machine gun and is spraying fire everywhere. In those cases, the best course of action might be to just duck down and let it go, survive to talk and create Positive Friction another day.

I'm sorry if I deceived you, but this book is really less about the raging Ego Monsters who you want to manage and control than it is about YOU. You control everything that goes on in your life. Not the other person. You can affect the outcome of every situation you're in, if you think before you react. If you fortify your Information Traffic Cop, so he's alert 24 hours a day, seven days a week, you can steer clear of all the Ego Flares, Ego Fires, Ego Explosions, and Ego Monsters in your life. Remember, ego is a ball of energy. Every ego is the same size. When information gets to your ego, there will be friction. Will it be positive or negative? When someone is yelling at you, will you yell back? Or will you "Give 'Em A Cookie?" What will you do when there is an Ego Flare right in front of you? Will you throw on gasoline, or water?

If you control your own ego, then you control your world. It doesn't matter what anyone else is doing, saying, or yelling. You don't care. You care about you. How will you react? Will you make the situation worse, or better? Can you create Positive Friction within yourself and give an Ego Monster a Cookie? Most people can't, but you're not 'most people' because you've read this book—so you can "Give 'Em A Cookie." Remember, it's okay if you sometimes have to duck, retreat, regroup, and/or leave.

Here's what I want you to do. Read the book again. It's only about 125 pages. This time when you read it, after you smile, laugh, cringe, or cry about the other person, think about yourself. Who are you in the story? What would you do in that situation to make it better? How would you create Positive Friction? I'm no PHD. I'm just a guy who has had the opportunity to interact with thousands of people close up, in stressful situations. I've made plenty of mistakes and handled many situations the wrong way. It's when I started to look within, and analyze why I was reacting in certain ways to situations, that I was able to break through. With only Positive Friction in your life, nothing can stop you. You can do anything you want to do. You can be anyone you want to be. The world is yours. Nothing can get in your way.

One more thing—What's with that shirt you're wearing? It's kinda loud. . . . .

-end-

How many Ego Monsters did you think of while reading this book? When I first started writing about egos, everyone I talked to said, "What a great subject! I can think of plenty of people that should read your book."

I thought it would be a good idea to give you, the reader, the opportunity to send *"The Little Book on Big Ego"* to anyone want you want....ANONYMOUSLY!

If sending your favorite Ego Monster this book doesn't do the situation justice, you can share your ego stories with me on my website. I will personally review your story and offer advice on how you can turn your ego scenario into a positive result.

Just log on to www.frictionfactor.net and you can submit your ego story, sign up for my free ezine, or purchase this book anonymously for that special Ego Monster in your life. I guarantee your identity will be protected. The Ego Monster will never know who sent them the book.

Thank you for reading "The Little Book on Big Ego"

Joel